D1230047

17.95

I Love Sports
Snowboarding
by Kaitlyn Duling

Bullfrog Books

Ideas for Parents and Teachers

Bullfrog Books let children practice reading informational text at the earliest reading levels. Repetition, familiar words, and photo labels support early readers.

Before Reading

- Discuss the cover photo. What does it tell them?

- Look at the picture glossary together. Read and discuss the words.

Read the Book

- "Walk" through the book and look at the photos. Let the child ask questions. Point out the photo labels.

- Read the book to the child, or have him or her read independently.

After Reading

- Prompt the child to think more. Ask: Have you ever been snowboarding? Did you enjoy it?

Bullfrog Books are published by Jump!
5357 Penn Avenue South
Minneapolis, MN 55419
www.jumplibrary.com

Library of Congress Cataloging-in-Publication Data

Names: Duling, Kaitlyn.
Title: Snowboarding / by Kaitlyn Duling.
Description: Minneapolis, Minnesota: Jump!, Inc., 2018. | Series: I love sports | Includes index.
Identifiers: LCCN 2017022932 (print) | LCCN 2017033289 (ebook) | ISBN 9781624966705 (ebook) ISBN 9781620318225 (hardcover: alk. paper)
Subjects: LCSH: Snowboarding—Juvenile literature.
Classification: LCC GV857.S57 (ebook) | LCC GV857. S57 D85 2017 (print) | DDC 796.939—dc23
LC record available at https://lccn.loc.gov/2017022932

Editor: Jenna Trnka
Book Designer: Leah Sanders
Photo Researcher: Leah Sanders

Photo Credits: George Rudy/Shutterstock, cover; KarenMower/iStock, 1; Janks/Dreamstime, 3; Sergey Novikov/Shutterstock, 4; SerrNovik/iStock, 5; Hero Images/Getty, 6–7; Max Topchii/Shutterstock, 8–9, 23tr; talevr/iStock, 10; Sergey Furtaev/Shutterstock, 11; Mirelle/Shutterstock, 12–13, 23br; MaxTopchii/iStock, 13; Arnold Media/Getty, 14–15; db2stock/Getty, 16–17, 23bl; 2xSamara.com/Shutterstock, 18, 23tl; Dmitry Molchanov/Shutterstock, 19; ChristopherBernard/iStock, 20–21; Oleksandr Rzhanitsyn/Shutterstock, 22; ppart/Shutterstock, 24.

Printed in the United States of America at Corporate Graphics in North Mankato, Minnesota.

Table of Contents

Let's Snowboard! 4

Snowboarding Gear 22

Picture Glossary 23

Index 24

To Learn More 24

Let's Snowboard!

Grab your gear.
There is fresh snow.

Let's snowboard!

Liv gets ready.

She puts on a coat.

She puts on
snow pants.

Mae wears a helmet.

She wears goggles.

Next, Mae puts on boots.

**They strap
to the board.**

She is ready!

lift

Dan rides the lift.

It is fun!

He can see far.

Zac is ready to go!

He bends his knees.

He shifts
his weight.

Off he goes!

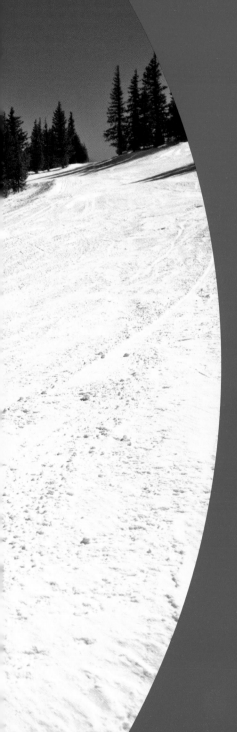

Lucy turns her body.

It turns the board, too.

Sam goes over a jump. He gets air!

Sam lands.

He goes
down the hill.

You can board, too.

Let's go!

Snowboarding Gear

helmet

goggles

coat

gloves

straps

snow pants

snowboard

boots

22

Picture Glossary

air
When you do a jump and your snowboard comes up off the snow.

helmet
A hard hat that is worn to protect your head.

goggles
Close-fitting plastic glasses. They protect the eyes from sun and snow.

lift
Moving seats that bring snowboarders to the top of a hill.

Index

board 11, 17

boots 10

coat 7

gear 4

goggles 8

helmet 8

hill 19

jump 18

lift 13

snow 4

snow pants 7

strap 11

To Learn More

Learning more is as easy as 1, 2, 3.

1) Go to www.factsurfer.com

2) Enter "snowboarding" into the search box.

3) Click the "Surf" button to see a list of websites.

With factsurfer.com, finding more information is just a click away.